THE GRACIOUS TABLE
DESSERTS BY CAROL

10 Gluten Free Cheesecakes

On the front cover:
(top left) Plain Cheesecake
(bottom right) Pumpkin Cheesecake

On the back cover:
Three views of Peach-Lime Cheesecake

Copyright ©CarTan 2020

ISBN 978-0-9696738-4-2

All rights reserved.

No part of this book may be reproduced in any form, by photocopy, microfilm, xerography, or any other means, or incorporated into any retrieval system, electronic or mechanical, without the written permission of the copyright owner.

Publisher: CarTan, Montreal, Canada
Photography: Carol Tansey
Layout Design: Jacqui Dawson

CONTENTS

CHEESECAKES BY CAROL 1

    Banana-Lime Cheesecake 3

    Cherry or Plain Cheesecake 5

    Kiwi-Raspberry or Mixed Fruit Cheesecake 8

    Orange Cheesecake 11

    Peach-Lime Cheesecake 13

    Pineapple Cheesecake 16

    Pumpkin Cheesecake 19

    Strawberry Cheesecake 21

    Raspberry Cheese Pie 23

    Kiwi-Pineapple Cheese Squares 25

GLUTEN FREE FLOUR MIX 27

ABOUT THE AUTHOR 28

CHEESECAKES

Not for every day, but oh so gorgeous for very special days

Ten cheesecakes are included in this cookbook—all must be prepared a day ahead of serving. All are cooked cheesecakes—so all need overnight chilling. In each case, the fruit topping should be put on shortly before serving.

Some of these cheesecakes are made with cream cheese, some with a combination of cream cheese and cottage cheese, while others include sour cream and whipping cream. The ones with cottage cheese and cream cheese are a little lighter than the ones with cream cheese alone—but these are richer and creamier. Sour cream, both in the cake and as a topping, adds a certain flair to the cake. The ones with whipping cream provide a richer flavour. Whichever you choose—they are all gorgeous.

I always put a cookie sheet on the bottom shelf of the oven—sometimes a cheesecake springform pan leaks a little. It is also wise to put in the oven a small pan of water to keep the cake from falling or cracking. Recipes for a pie and for squares are also included along with the more traditional cheesecakes.

There are different ways of measuring cream cheese:

1 1/2 lbs cream cheese = 2 4/5 large packages

1 lb = 1 4/5 large packages

454 grams = 1 lb

THE GRACIOUS TABLE: DESSERTS BY CAROL

BANANA-LIME CHEESECAKE

BANANA-LIME CHEESECAKE
8-INCH SPRINGFORM PAN, BUTTERED

Base

1 cup	gluten free cracker crumbs
1/2 cup	powdered almonds
1/4 cup	sugar
1/2 teaspoon	cinnamon
6 Tablespoons	melted butter

- Mix together crumbs, powdered almonds, sugar and cinnamon. Stir in melted butter.
- Press mixture into buttered 8-inch springform pan and bake in preheated 350° oven for 10 minutes.
- Cool to room temperature for 10 minutes, then chill in freezer for 10 minutes.

Filling

1 4/5 pkgs (450g)	cream cheese
1/2 cup	brown sugar
juice of 2	limes
2	medium mashed bananas
4	large eggs
1 cup	sour cream

- In mixer, beat together cream cheese and brown sugar until light and creamy.
- Add lime juice and mashed bananas and beat. Add eggs, 1 at a time, continuing to beat until light.
- Add sour cream and beat one minute more until blended together.
- Pour mixture over prepared base and bake in preheated 350° oven for 60-70 minutes or until centre is firm. Turn oven off and allow cake to dry in oven with door slightly open for 30 minutes. Cool to room temperature before refrigerating for several hours or overnight.

BANANA-LIME CHEESECAKE
CONTINUED

TOPPING

for sifting	icing sugar
2	bananas
juice of 1	lime
juice of 1	lemon

- Shortly before serving, remove sides of springform pan. Sift icing sugar over top of cake.

- Cut banana slices and soak in lime-lemon juice for a few minutes, making sure all slices are juice-coated.

- Place banana slices around top of cake and in centre. Sift a little more icing sugar over top of cake.

- Place cake (still on bottom of pan) onto a paper doily on cake platter. Refrigerate until serving time.

This is a delicious cake—the tastes of lime and banana are quite distinct. It cuts very cleanly and serves nicely. It is a little heavier than some cheesecakes, so needs only a small piece per serving. It becomes even tastier after a day or two.

10 Gluten Free Cheesecakes

CHERRY CHEESECAKE

CHERRY OR PLAIN CHEESECAKE
10 1/4-INCH SPRINGFORM PAN, BUTTERED

BASE

1 1/2 cups	gluten free crumbs
1/4 cup	sugar
1 teaspoon	cinnamon
6 Tablespoons	melted sweet butter

- Mix thoroughly: crumbs, sugar and cinnamon. Stir in melted butter. Press mixture into the bottom of 10 1/4-inch springform pan.
- Bake for 10 minutes in preheated 325° oven, then remove from oven. Keep at room temperature for 10 minutes, then place in freezer for 10 minutes.

CHERRY OR PLAIN CHEESECAKE
CONTINUED

FILLING

1/8 teaspoon	cream of tartar
5	large eggs *(separated)*
1/2 cup	sugar
3 teaspoons	lemon juice
1 lb	cream cheese
2 cups	sour cream

- Add cream of tartar to egg whites and beat until soft peaks form. Gradually add sugar and beat until stiff peaks form. Set aside.

- In a large bowl, with mixer, beat cream cheese until it is light and smooth. Add lemon juice and beat some more. Add egg yolks, one at a time, beating after each. Then stir in sour cream gently and fold in beaten egg whites. Pour into prepared crust.

- Bake for 1 hour and 10-15 minutes in preheated 325° oven until centre feels firm to the touch and cake is set.

- Turn off oven and leave cake in oven to dry out for about 20-30 minutes. (If oven is electric, leave oven door slightly ajar while in drying-out period.)

- Remove from oven and cool to room temperature on wire rack. After about 15-20 minutes, loosen sides carefully with knife (do not remove sides of springform pan yet). Refrigerate.

PLAIN CHEESECAKE

CHERRY OR PLAIN CHEESECAKE
CONTINUED

CHERRY TOPPING

14 oz can	Bing cherries
1 Tablespoon	corn starch
2 Tablespoons	sugar
4 teaspoons	lemon juice

- Drain cherries, reserving 3/4 cup of the liquid. Pit the cherries.
- Mix together corn starch and sugar in small saucepan.
- Add reserved liquid from cherries and lemon juice and place over medium heat.
- Bring to boil and let cook for 5 minutes.
- Pour over pitted cherries and allow to cool.
- When cake and cherry topping are both thoroughly chilled, remove cake from refrigerator. Release sides of pan and place cake on paper doily on platter (leaving bottom of pan under cake).
- Spread cherry topping over top of cake and refrigerate until serving time.

PLAIN CHEESECAKE TOPPING

for sifting	icing sugar

- Omit making CHERRY TOPPING. You need only some icing sugar.
- When cake is thoroughly chilled—after several hours or overnight in refrigerator—sift icing sugar over top of cake and refrigerate until serving time.

This is the lightest of the cheesecakes in the book.
For lightness and taste, this is my favourite.

THE GRACIOUS TABLE: DESSERTS BY CAROL

KIWI-RASPBERRY OR MIXED FRUIT CHEESECAKE

KIWI-RASPBERRY OR MIXED FRUIT CHEESECAKE
9-INCH SPRINGFORM PAN, BUTTERED

BASE

1 1/3 cups	gluten free crumbs
3 Tablespoons	sugar
1/2 teaspoon	cinnamon
6 Tablespoons	melted butter

- Mix together crumbs, cinnamon and sugar. Stir in melted butter.
- Press into buttered 9-inch springform pan. Set aside.

Filling

2 4/5 pkgs (700g)	cream cheese
2 Tablespoons	milk
1/4 teaspoon	salt
1 teaspoon	vanilla
4	large eggs *(beaten)*
1 cup	sugar

- Beat together cream cheese, milk, salt and vanilla until thoroughly blended. Add beaten eggs and sugar, and continue to beat until creamy.

- Pour mixture onto base and bake in preheated 350° oven for 45-55 minutes or until cake is set in centre.

- **Remove from oven and cool for 10 minutes. *Do not turn oven off.***

Topping

1 cup	sour cream
3 Tablespoons	icing sugar
1/2 teaspoon	vanilla
5	kiwis *(peeled and sliced)*

fresh raspberries, canned mandarin orange slices or other fruit of your choice

- Mix together sour cream, icing sugar, and vanilla. Spread over top of cheesecake.

- Return cheesecake to oven and continue to bake for 15 minutes.

- Remove from oven, cool to room temperature and then refrigerate for several hours or overnight.

- Shortly before serving, remove sides of springform pan. Place cake (still on bottom of pan) onto doily on cake plate and decorate with kiwis, raspberries, mandarin orange slices or other fruit of your choice. Return to refrigerator until serving time.

This is an absolutely gorgeous cake—rich, creamy, delicious and cuts cleanly.

THE GRACIOUS TABLE: DESSERTS BY CAROL

ORANGE CHEESECAKE

ORANGE CHEESECAKE
10 1/4-INCH SPRINGFORM PAN, BUTTERED

BASE

1 1/2 cups	gluten free crumbs
1/4 cup	sugar
1 teaspoon	cinnamon
7 Tablespoons	melted sweet butter

- Mix together thoroughly: crumbs, sugar, and cinnamon. Stir in melted butter.

- Press into bottom of buttered 10 1/4-inch springform pan.

- Bake at 375° for 7-10 minutes. Cool to room temperature for 10 minutes, then place in freezer for 10 minutes.

FILLING

1/4 cup	gluten free flour mix
1/4 teaspoon	baking powder
5	large eggs
1 2/3 cups	dry cottage cheese
1 1/3 cups	cream cheese
1 cup	sugar
3 teaspoons	orange juice
1 cup	sour cream
1/8 teaspoon	cream of tartar

- Sift flour and baking powder together. Set aside.

- Separate yolks and whites of eggs. Set aside.

- Place dry cottage cheese, cream cheese and sugar in food processor and process until smooth. Add flour mixture and orange juice and process. Add egg yolks, sour cream, and process. Set aside.

(continued on next page)

ORANGE CHEESECAKE
CONTINUED

FILLING

(continued from previous page)

- In a separate bowl and with mixer, beat egg whites with cream of tartar until they form stiff peaks, then fold them into cheese mixture.

- Pour mixture into prepared crust—to 3/4 inch from top of pan—and bake in preheated 350° oven for 35-45 minutes or until centre is firm and cake is just beginning to brown.

- Turn off oven. Leave cake in oven to dry for one hour. *(If oven is electric, leave oven door slightly ajar for 20-25 minutes to let some heat escape, then close door for balance of hour).*

- Remove cake from oven, cool to room temperature, then refrigerate for several hours.

TOPPING

2 Tablespoons	sweet butter
2/3 cup	sugar
2	eggs *(beaten)*
2 Tablespoons	orange juice
10 oz can	mandarin oranges

- Melt butter, then stir sugar, beaten eggs and 2 Tablespoons orange juice into the pan. Cook until thick. *(Will be thick when mixture comes to boil and boils gently for 2 minutes.)* Cool.

- When both cake and topping are thoroughly chilled, remove sides of pan *(keep cake on bottom of pan)* and place on doily on cake plate. Spread topping over cake and refrigerate overnight.

- 2 to 3 hours before serving, place drained orange sections around top of cake decoratively and return to refrigerator until serving time.

This is a delicious light cheesecake.

PEACH-LIME CHEESECAKE
10 1/4-INCH SPRINGFORM PAN, BUTTERED

PEACH-LIME CHEESECAKE

BASE

1 1/2 cups	gluten free crumbs
1/4 cup	sugar
1/2 teaspoon	cinnamon
6 Tablespoons	melted butter

- Mix together crumbs, sugar and cinnamon. Stir in melted butter.
- Press into buttered 10 1/4-inch springform pan.
- Bake in preheated 350° oven for 10 minutes, cool to room temperature for 10 minutes, then chill in freezer for 10 minutes.

PEACH-LIME CHEESECAKE
CONTINUED

FILLING

2 4/5 pkgs (700 g)	cream cheese
1 2/3 cups	icing sugar
1 Tablespoon	gluten free potato starch
1/8 teaspoon	cream of tartar
7	eggs *(separated)*
2 cups	sour cream
2 teaspoons	fresh lime juice

- Beat together cream cheese, sugar and potato starch until smooth and creamy. Add egg yolks, 1 at a time, beating after each addition. Set aside.

- With clean beaters, in a separate bowl, beat egg whites and cream of tartar until stiff peaks form. Set aside.

- Stir sour cream and lime juice into cheese mixture. Gently fold in egg whites. Pour over prepared base and bake for about 90 minutes, or until centre is firm, in preheated 275° oven.

- Turn oven off and leave cake in oven to dry for 2 hours, with oven door slightly open. Then cool to room temperature before refrigerating.

PEACH-LIME CHEESECAKE
CONTINUED

Peach Preserve Topping

9	peaches *(peeled, sliced)*
2 Tablespoons	fresh lime juice
1 cup	sugar

- Mix together the peaches, sugar and lime juice and bring mixture to the boil. Cook for 10 minutes or until jam stage is reached *(when a drop sets on a cold saucer)*.

- Remove mixture from heat, place in a bowl, and let cool to room temperature. Then cover and refrigerate.

- Shortly before serving, remove sides of springform pan *(keeping cake on bottom of pan)*. Place cake onto doily on cake platter.

- Spread topping over cake and return to refrigerator until served.

This is a rich, creamy cheesecake.

PINEAPPLE CHEESECAKE
10 1/4-INCH SPRINGFORM PAN, BUTTERED

BASE

1 1/2 cups	gluten free crumbs
1/4 cup	sugar
1/2 teaspoon	cinnamon
6 Tablespoons	melted butter

- Mix together crumbs, sugar and cinnamon. Stir in melted butter.

- Press mixture into buttered 10 1/4-inch springform pan.

- Bake in preheated 350° oven for 10 minutes. Cool to room temperature for 10 minutes, then chill in freezer for 10 minutes.

FILLING

2 4/5 pkgs (700g)	cream cheese
1 2/3 cups	icing sugar
1 Tablespoon	potato starch
7	eggs *(separated)*
1/8 teaspoon	cream of tartar
2 cups	sour cream
2 teaspoons	fresh lime juice

- Beat together cream cheese, sugar and potato starch until smooth and creamy. Add egg yolks—1 at a time—beating after each addition. Set aside.

- With clean beaters, in a separate bowl, beat egg whites and cream of tartar until stiff peaks form. Set aside.

- Stir sour cream and lime juice into cheese mixture. Gently fold in egg whites.

- Pour over prepared base and bake for about 90 minutes—or until centre is firm—in preheated 275° oven.

- Turn oven off and leave cake in oven to dry for 2 hours—with oven door slightly open. Then cool to room temperature and refrigerate.

10 Gluten Free Cheesecakes

PINEAPPLE CHEESECAKE

Topping

1 can	crushed pineapple
1 teaspoon	cinnamon

- Open can of crushed pineapple and drain liquid. Chill fruit in refrigerator.
- Mix crushed pineapple with cinnamon and decorate top of cake. Return to refrigerator until serving time.

This is a gentle delicious cheesecake.

THE GRACIOUS TABLE: DESSERTS BY CAROL

PUMPKIN CHEESECAKE

PUMPKIN CHEESECAKE
10 1/4-inch springform pan, buttered

Base

2 cups	gluten free crumbs
1/2 cup	powdered almonds
1/2 cup	sugar
1/4 cup	light cream
1/2 cup	melted butter
1/2 teaspoon	cinnamon

- Mix all ingredients together and spread in buttered 10 1/4-inch springform pan.
- Cook in preheated 325° oven for 20 minutes, then place in freezer for 10 minutes.

Filling

4 cups	cream cheese
7/8 cup	sugar
4	eggs
2	egg yolks
2 2/3 Tablespoons	gluten free potato starch
1 teaspoon	ginger
1 teaspoon	cloves
1 Tablespoon	vanilla
7/8 cup	whipping cream
1 3/4 cups	mashed pumpkin

- Beat together: cream cheese, sugar, eggs and egg yolks. Add potato starch, cinnamon, ginger, cloves and vanilla. Beat again.
- Beat in whipping cream. Add mashed pumpkin and beat again. Pour mixture into prepared crust.

(continued on next page)

PUMPKIN CHEESECAKE
CONTINUED

FILLING

(continued from previous page)

- Preheat oven to 425° and bake for 15 minutes. Reduce heat to 275° and continue to bake for 1 hour. Turn heat off and leave cake in oven for about 2 hours to dry out.

- If your oven is electric, and you are sure that cake is thoroughly cooked, turn oven off and open door slightly for first 30-45 minutes. If cake is not thoroughly cooked, then leave it cooking, but do not open oven door until it is finished. Then let it dry out in oven with oven door slightly ajar for about 30 minutes.

- Once dried out, cool cake at room temperature for 1-2 hours, then refrigerate.

- Serve as is or with either whipped cream or ice cream. Cut in very small pieces as this cake, though delicious, is very rich and a little goes a long way. It cuts easily and cleanly.

One of my official tasters, the friend of a relative, claims the PUMPKIN CHEESECAKE as his favourite of all the cheesecakes. I am also very fond of it.

STRAWBERRY CHEESECAKE
9-INCH SPRINGFORM PAN, BUTTERED

STRAWBERRY CHEESECAKE

BASE

1 1/3 cups	gluten free crumbs
3 Tablespoons	sugar
1/2 teaspoon	cinnamon
6 Tablespoons	melted butter

- Mix together crumbs, sugar and cinnamon. Stir in melted butter.
- Press into buttered 9-inch springform pan. Set aside.

STRAWBERRY CHEESECAKE
CONTINUED

FILLING

2 4/5 pkgs (700g)	cream cheese
2 Tablespoons	milk
1/4 teaspoon	salt
1 teaspoon	vanilla
4	large eggs *(beaten)*
1 cup	sugar

- Beat together cream cheese, milk, salt and vanilla until thoroughly blended. Add beaten eggs and sugar, and continue to beat until creamy.

- Pour mixture onto base and bake in preheated 350° oven for 45-55 minutes or until cake is set in center. Remove from oven and cool for 10 minutes. *(Do not turn oven off—but do remove cake).*

TOPPING

1 cup	sour cream
3 Tablespoons	icing sugar
1/2 teaspoon	vanilla

- Mix together sour cream, icing sugar and vanilla and spread over cheesecake. Return to oven and continue to bake for 15 minutes. Remove from oven, cool to room temperature and refrigerate for several hours or overnight.

- Shortly before serving, remove sides of springform pan. Place cake (still on bottom of pan) onto doily on cake plate and decorate with strawberries made into jam. Return to refrigerator until serving time.

For strawberry jam:

1/2 cup	maple syrup
small box	fresh strawberries
1/2 cup	water

- Pick over and wash strawberries. Place strawberries, water, and maple syrup into a pan. Bring to a boil and simmer for 5-7 minutes—until a soft ball is formed when tested on a cold saucer and strawberries are soft. Chill to room temperature, then refrigerate. Pour over cake at serving time.

I served this for my sister's 80th Birthday—it was a big success.

10 Gluten Free Cheesecakes

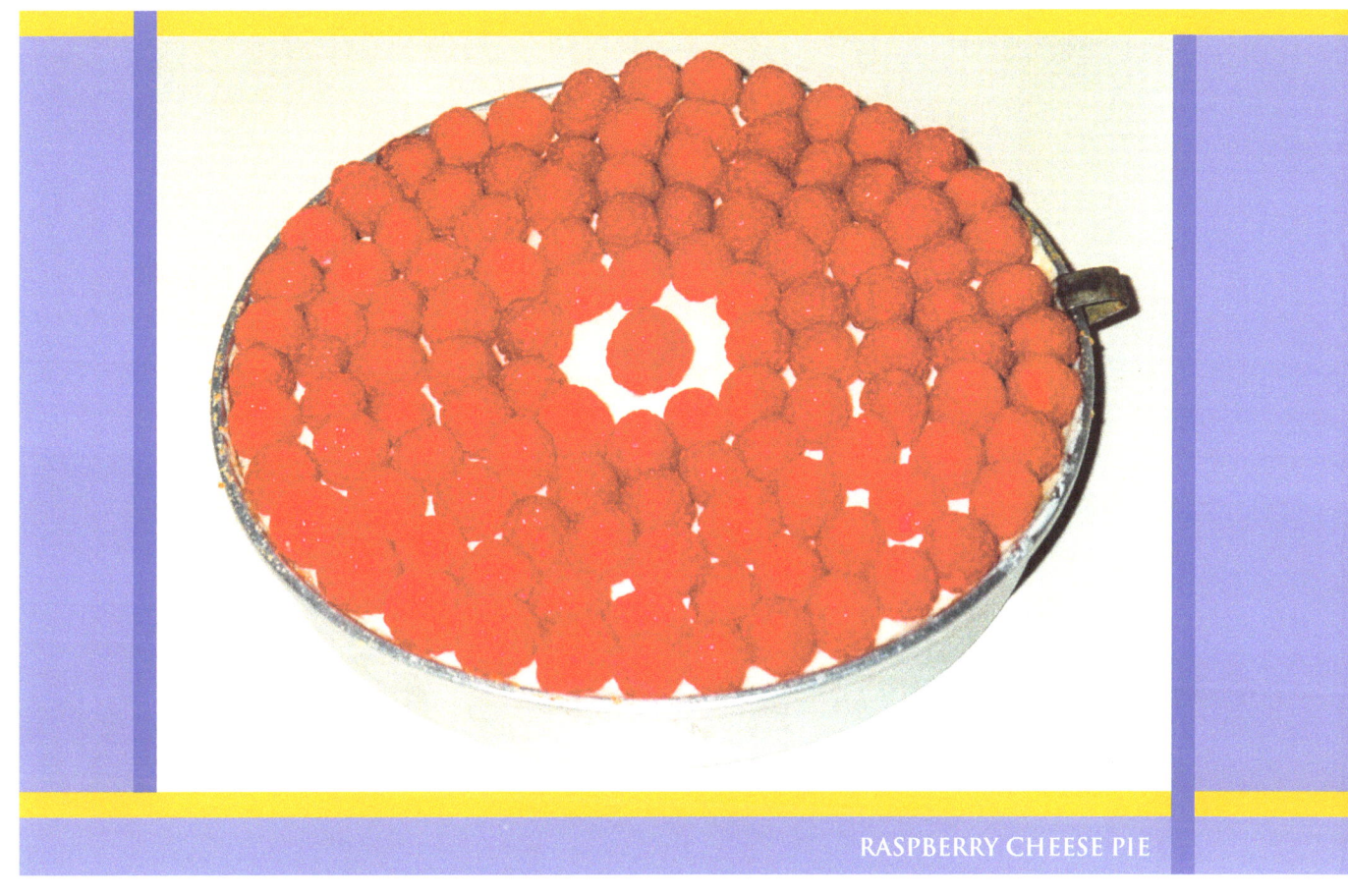

RASPBERRY CHEESE PIE

RASPBERRY CHEESE PIE
9-INCH ROUND PIE PLATE/PAN, BUTTERED

BASE

1 1/4 cups	gluten free crumbs
2 Tablespoons	sugar
1/2 teaspoon	cinnamon
4 Tablespoons	melted butter

- Mix together crumbs, sugar and cinnamon and stir in melted butter. Press into bottom of buttered 9-inch round pie plate.
- Bake in preheated 350° oven for 10 minutes. Cool to room temperature for 10 minutes. Set aside.

RASPBERRY CHEESE PIE
CONTINUED

FILLING

1 1/2 pkgs (350g)	cream cheese
1 cup	sugar
1 cup	fresh raspberries
4	eggs
1 teaspoon	vanilla

- Cream together cream cheese and sugar. Add eggs, 1 at a time, and beat after addition of each. Add vanilla and mix. Fold in raspberries.
- Pour mixture onto prepared base and bake in preheated 350° oven for 45-50 minutes—until centre is firm. Remove from oven and cool for 15 minutes. *(Do not turn oven off)*.

TOPPING

1 cup	sour cream
3 Tablespoons	icing sugar
6-12 oz	fresh raspberries

- Mix sour cream and icing sugar together and spread over pie. Return to oven and bake for 15 minutes.
- Cool pie to room temperature, then refrigerate for several hours.
- Shortly before serving, decorate top of pie with fresh raspberries.

Delicious—but very rich and heavy—so need only a small piece.

KIWI-PINEAPPLE CHEESE SQUARES
8X8-INCH SQUARE PAN OR ROUND SPRINGFORM PAN, BUTTERED

KIWI-PINEAPPLE CHEESE SQUARES

BASE

3/4 cup	brown rice flour mix
1/4 cup	ground almonds
1/2 teaspoon	cinnamon
1/4 cup	coconut
2 Tablespoons	sugar
4 Tablespoons	melted butter

- Mix all ingredients together. Reserve a half cup for topping. Lay mixture in 8x8 inch buttered pan. Cover with filling (see next page). Sprinkle reserved half cup of base mixture on top.

KIWI-PINEAPPLE CHEESE SQUARES
CONTINUED

FILLING

1 cup/8 oz pkg/250g	cream cheese
2	large eggs
2/3 cup	crushed pineapple *(well drained)*
3	kiwis *(peeled, chopped)*
1/2 cup	sugar
1 teaspoon	vanilla
pinch of	salt

- In mixer, cream together cream cheese and sugar. Add eggs and beat. Add vanilla and salt and beat. Fold in drained pineapple and chopped kiwis.
- Lay mixture on prepared base and sprinkle top with half cup of reserved base mixture, as directed previously.
- Bake in preheated 350° degree oven for 35-40 minutes, until cheese filling is firm to touch and topping is lightly browned. Cool and refrigerate.

CUT ONLY WHEN COOL.

Variation: You can use an additional 1 cup drained crushed pineapple if kiwis are unavailable.

Makes 25 squares.

These are lovely—each square a delicious refreshing cheesecake by itself.

GLUTEN FREE FLOUR MIX

    1 cup / 250g   white/brown rice flour
    5 Tbls / 75g   potato starch flour
    2 1/2 Tbls / 37g   tapioca flour

- Mix the 3 flours together. Save in freezer.
- Use when called for in different recipes.

About the Author

Carol Tansey claims that food is her passion. She studied Nutrition at Macdonald College of McGill University in Montreal, Canada. Then, in her fifties, she returned to McGill University for seven years (nights and weekends) to follow a Certificate Program in Management in Health and Social Services. At the time she was working in a Seniors' Residence which was becoming Government Administered and Government Funded from having been only 80% funded. Through all this her interest has always been to keep people eating and enjoying healthful food.

Books by Carol Tansey:

The Gracious Table: Desserts by Carol

The Gracious Table: Soups by Carol, *100 Gluten Free Soups*

The Gracious Table: Dinners by Carol, *43 Gluten Free Dinners*

Prognosis for a Septuagenarian/Octogenarian

The Gracious Table: Desserts by Carol *10 Gluten Free Cheesecakes*

www.ingramcontent.com/pod-product-compliance
Lightning Source LLC
LaVergne TN
LVHW072105070426
835508LV00003B/274